FAIRACRES PUBLICATIONS 237

PEOPLE WITH DEMENTIA AS TEACHERS OF FAITH

Regina Schlingheider

Fairacres Publications 237

ISBN 978-0-7283-0508-3
Fairacres Publications Series ISSN 0307-1405

The publishers have no control over, or responsibility for, any third-party website referred to in this book. All internet addresses given in this book were correct at the time of going to press. The authors and publisher regret any inconvenience caused if addresses have changed or sites have ceased to exist, but can accept no responsibility for any such changes.

Edited and typeset in Palatino Linotype by Julia Craig-McFeely

Cover image by Sister Rosemary SLG

SLG Press
Convent of the Incarnation
Fairacres • Oxford
www.slgpress.co.uk

Printed by
Grosvenor Group Ltd, Loughton, Essex

SLG Press Publications are printed on FSC Certified sustainable papers.

CONTENTS

People with Dementia as Teachers of Faith

Introduction

Not long ago, on the bus, I met a man from my church who is in the early stages of dementia, and when we talked, it came as a surprise that our conversation was so easy. He had always been an exacting man, strict with himself and with others. Now he showed genuine joy to see me, and we talked easily, unconcerned whether every sentence made sense. When we fell silent, it did not feel awkward. When I got off the bus I felt refreshed rather than strained by this encounter and realized that this was different from our meetings before he developed dementia.

Dementia is dreaded in our society, and many of us would rather live with severe physical impairments than lose our minds. To most of us, the story of dementia is essentially a story of loss and decline. Dementia *is* a burden, and it causes much suffering, not only for those with dementia, but also for those who live with them and care for them. However, I believe that in the midst of the hardships it causes it is possible to look beyond the ostensible facts to something hopeful. God speaks to us through people with cognitive impairment and challenges our assumption that to believe in him we must have a sound mind. People with dementia teach us theology, they *live* teachings of the Bible and make us see particular Bible verses in a new light.

People with dementia contribute to our Christian spirituality, not in so many words but by living and being with their illness. In this book I present five aspects by which they show us that cognitive impairment may open up new ways of understanding God and faith:

—despite our emphasis in Western societies on autonomy and self-reliance, being a burden can be a calling and is often gracefully accepted by people with dementia;

—their handing over of their lives to others shows carers a new dimension of trust;

—there is enjoyment in their lives, and their cognitive impairment can lead to a life with fewer worries;

—forgetfulness may open up ways to new relationships and to being together in a less demanding fashion;

—by meeting the dead in their parallel world, people with dementia can also teach about death.

If God is the Word that 'became flesh' (John 1:14), there must be other ways of knowing him, apart from knowing *about* him. By God's grace, people with dementia can lead lives of faith and express their trust in God in their own special ways. When we are with them, we can learn something about faith and prayer. Without wanting to dismiss the hardship experienced by people with dementia and their carers, the main focus of this book will be on hopeful moments in this hardship. There is a spirituality which we may miss out on if we do not pay attention to what people with dementia can teach us. The church should stop seeing them merely as sufferers in need of our pastoral attention and instead start valuing them as teachers of faith.

Nowhere in the Bible will we find an explanation for the suffering of people with dementia and their carers. The book of Job asks the question: 'Why do people suffer?', but does not provide an answer; the 'wound is kept open'.[1] When he loses his children, his property and his health, Job's friends search for a reason for his suffering. If they can find an explanation, they may be able to convince themselves that they cannot be struck in the same way. In their eyes, Job must have done something to deserve these blows of fate.[2] But Job remains stubborn: I am not guilty. What happens to me is not a punishment. There is no explanation.

> But he knows the way that I take;
> when he has tested me, I shall come out like gold.
> My foot has held fast to his steps;
> I have kept his way and have not turned aside.
> I have not departed from the commandment of his lips;
> I have treasured in my bosom the words of his mouth.
>
> (Job 23:10–12)

Job is not just the object of his friends' efforts to make sense of his suffering. He makes his own voice heard, and he keeps talking to God. He has not given up on God, and although he feels 'fenced in' (Job 3:23) and wonders if there is any sense in

---

[1] Ralph Kunz, 'Das Schicksal Demenz und Hiobs Botschaft', in *Kulturen der Sorge: Wie eine Gesellschaft ein Leben mit Demenz ermöglichen kann,* ed. Harm-Peer Zimmermann (Campus Verlag, 2018), 157.

[2] See e.g. Job 22.

going on living he is not overcome completely by his suffering. He remains a subject, a person, in his lament and in his struggle with God. In his suffering, he does not lose his dignity.[3] Often, people with dementia are reduced to the fact that they have this disease, they are defined and diminished by it. This makes it hard to see other aspects of their lives and remember that dementia is not the most important piece of information about a person. Sharon Waller wrote about her father:

> The condition of Alzheimer's was used as identification, as a reason, and as a predictor … It provided reason enough to speak and act in a certain way and not another. It defined the quality of many of his interactions. My father's dementia was at least as much socially and culturally constructed as it was medically defined.[4]

How does dementia affect our social lives? Once we have become people with dementia, does it label us in every other aspect of our lives? Is there nothing left, apart from dementia? At a church group of elderly people that I meet once a week, one of the ladies failed to come for a while. When she returned she was brought by her daughter. While she was taking off her coat, her daughter, from a distance, mouthed the word 'Dementia!' in my direction. I knew the mother had been struggling with her memory, and to be told just this one word about her condition somehow did not seem right. It seemed to diminish her and seemed to turn her from the person I knew into an object, a mere object of dementia.

Job, however, is not an object. The story we are told about him in the Bible ensures his illness and grief are not the only information about him. He is still someone in relationship to God,

---

[3] Kunz, 'Hiobs Botschaft', 161.

[4] Cited in Malcolm Goldsmith, *In a Strange Land: People with Dementia and the Local Church* (4M Publications, 2004), 19–20.

his life story is not finished, he is not dead yet. He is sure that he has not done anything that makes him deserve becoming ill. In every severe illness we ask: 'Why should this happen to me?' but sense there will be no answer. Sickness is no respecter of persons, and God does not explain why we get ill. But the story of Job points to the fact that God does not abandon us, he is still there when we go through hardship and pain. We can talk to him and accuse him, and he is still present with us. We are asked to trust that he will not ask anything of us that he is not prepared to endure himself.[5] But this is hard for us, and we resent the fact that God does not give us an explanation.

Dignity in Dementia

In his book *The Old King in his Exile,* Arno Geiger reflects on his father's dementia. Describing it as a form of exile he takes his father's experience seriously, even if there is decline and strange behaviour. From their point of view, people with dementia have every right to behave in the way they do, because they have entered a different world, a 'strange land' which at first they do not understand. They must try to navigate this new world; they must survive without many things they relied on before. In a religious sense they must survive without the Temple, like the Israelites in exile in Babylon.[6] This strange or 'foreign land' referred to in

---

[5] This is reminiscent of Dietrich Bonhoeffer's refusal to believe in a *deus ex machina,* a God who miraculously delivers from harm. By being forced to live through the hardships as a political prisoner he found that God's help was not confined to sudden rescue operations. He experienced a closeness to him which had a different quality: 'Only the suffering God can help.' See Dietrich Bonhoeffer, *Letters and Papers from Prison,* Dietrich Bonhoeffer Works in English vol. 8, ed. John W. de Gruchy, trans. Isabel Best, Lisa E. Dahill, Reinhard Krauss and Nancy Lukens (Fortress Press, 2010), 479.

[6] See Goldsmith, *In a Strange Land,* 14.

Psalm 137:4 is a challenging place, not only because the Hebrew people are captive to the Babylonians. They also think they have lost their God, whose presence for them is tied to the Temple. But their time in exile becomes invaluable to them, as they discover that God *is* present there, in new and exciting ways. They have tasks in that land,[7] they are comforted and sustained by God who may not live in a building but can make 'the rough places a plain.' (Is. 40:4)

In a similar fashion, the vulnerability and captivity of dementia may be seen not merely as loss and abandonment, but as a chance of experiencing something new, something that gives rise to hope. Geiger's book shows moments in which the son was able to enter that strange land, and in which he and his father made sense of it as best they could. While doing this, they experienced precious moments of closeness. Dementia is usually seen as an illness that severs connections, but Arno Geiger's experience was that sometimes new connections are formed:

> the distance that had grown between my father and me was closing again, and ... we weren't losing touch, which is what I had long feared from the illness. Instead, there was an uncomplicated warmth between us, thanks to his forgetfulness, so that I almost welcomed this failing.[8]

Moreover, the closeness of death made the son feel moments of happiness with greater intensity. The book relates dialogues between son and father that show a sense of humour and, at times, unexpected depth and poetry. Again and again, the distance is bridged by unexpected gestures.

---

[7] See Jer. 29:7.

[8] Arno Geiger, *The Old King in his Exile*, trans. Stefan Tobler (Carl Hansler Verlag, 2013), 72–3. A more literal translation would render the last part: 'We made friends again, with a naturalness we owed to forgetting.'

Once, when I gave him my hand, he said how sorry he was that it was cold. I told him that I'd just been out in the rain. He held my hand between his two and said, 'Do whatever you need to be doing, but right now, I'm going to warm this hand.'[9]

Geiger realizes that, for his father, there is no other world apart from the world of dementia. He cannot cross the bridge into his son's world, which means the son has to move towards him and to some extent accept his father's muddled reality. He notices that by entering his father's world some of the bitterness of dementia is taken away, and he realizes that there, across the bridge,

> within the limits of his own mental state, beyond the wider society based on objectivity and linear goals, he is still an impressive man, and although not always very sensible by common standards, somehow brilliant.[10]

Geiger is able to see his father as someone, who is, although exiled and impaired, a person of importance and dignity. He is a king.

David Keck describes dementia as 'deconstruction incarnate'.[11] In the course of it you may lose the ability to walk and to recognize family members, and there may be a total loss of communication. In end-stage dementia, you may not be able to control grunting noises, screams, or seizures, and you may become incontinent.[12] Keck tries to imagine what it must be like for people with dementia to lose more and more of their original selves. Does it feel like extreme drunkenness? Is it a 'post-linguistic terror'?[13] Shifts in speaking and not finding the right words can be taken as jokes initially. In Emma Healey's book

---

[9] Geiger, *The Old King in his Exile*, 180.

[10] Geiger, *The Old King in his Exile*, 13.

[11] David Keck, *Forgetting Whose We Are: Alzheimer's Disease and the Love of God* (Abingdon Press, 1996), 37.

[12] Keck, *Forgetting Whose We Are*, 24.

[13] Keck, *Forgetting Whose We Are*, 28.

Elizabeth is Missing, the narrator, Maud, a woman with dementia, often describes objects by their properties when she cannot remember what they are called. When she wants to make toast she puts the bread in 'the bread-heater, the bread-browner.'[14] This literary device contributes to the fun of reading the book, but the fun is mixed with sadness about Maud losing her faculty of speech. The loss of control in language becomes less and less funny as dementia progresses, and can indeed become very ugly. Keck describes his mother, who had always been careful to control her anger, as cursing frequently.[15] Ann Johnson, a former nurse who was looked after by her mother when she became ill with early-onset dementia, says that they got on very well for about three years. Then one day her mother asked her not to speak to her 'like that.' Ann had developed behaviour problems and was using bad language, without being aware she was doing so.[16] Partners and close relations may live through months and years watching their loved ones change and decline and may have to cope with verbal and physical abuse.

The film *Still Alice* depicts clearly the mounting fear of the protagonist, a Linguistics professor teaching at university, as she struggles with early-onset dementia. Watching her bewilderment as she cannot remember what she is going to talk about in front of her students is deeply disturbing.[17] Clever direction in the film *The Father* makes the viewers experience things from the protagonist's perspective. Like Anthony, a man with dementia, they are confused about which place they are in or which person

---

[14] Emma Healey, *Elizabeth is Missing* (Penguin, 2015), 82.

[15] Keck, *Forgetting Whose We Are*, 32.

[16] Lucy Whitman, ed., *People with Dementia Speak Out* (Jessica Kingsley Publishers, 2016), 165.

[17] *Still Alice*, directed by Richard Glatzer and Wash Westmoreland (Killer Films and others, 2014), 1:39. Based on the novel of the same name by the neuroscientist Lisa Genova (iUniverse Pocket Books, 2007).

they are talking to. This film brings the plight of people with dementia into the lives of those who do not have contact with it, and shows the importance of trying to enter their world, increasingly chaotic as it may be.[18]

This is not an easy task. Restlessness, aggressiveness, unjust accusations and other forms of disturbing behaviour are difficult to deal with, and it is hard not to get angry with a person who is aggressive towards you. However, aggression and other forms of unusual behaviour often have a reason: it can be an illness or pain unknown to those around, or being in some way uncomfortable without being able to communicate it; it can be exasperation at not being able to say or do something that is important; it can be a daily routine the person is used to and is not able to abandon. Malcolm Goldsmith describes the example of a man in a care home who seemed to have a problem every morning. When staff found out that he had been a shepherd in the Scottish highlands and had been off extremely early every day to tend to his flock, they involved him in early morning tasks, before the day started for the other residents.[19]

Seeing people not just as a prey to dementia but as royals in exile, as people with an important life story and an inherent dignity, will help us to see behind what troubles them and can make relationships possible in unforeseen ways.

Memory

To some extent, all relationships are about entering the world of the other, and with people who have dementia this is often a rather strange world. Memory is central in Christian living; in

---

[18] *The Father*, directed by Florian Zeller (Les Films du Cru and others, 2020).

[19] Malcom Goldsmith, *In a Strange Land*, 44. On page 45 he lists more reasons behind physical aggressiveness or verbal abuse.

every church service Christians remember in liturgy, songs and prayers what Christ has done for them. In the Eucharist particularly, they recall and re-enact 'the night when he was betrayed' (1 Cor. 11:23) and with it other meals Jesus shared, his life, death, and resurrection. Does Christianity as a religion of remembrance lose its identity in the face of dementia?[20] Perhaps people with dementia help us to discover types of memory of which we are not commonly aware.

Vicarious Memory

The Church's memory is more long-lived than that of other institutions.[21] This long-term memory makes sure that God is not forgotten even if some of its members seem to forget him. Those without dementia remember and praise God on behalf of those with dementia and in this way follow Paul's exhortation: 'Bear one another's burdens' (Gal. 6:2). People with dementia are being taken up into a communal memory, not only by those around them in a church service, but also by those who have remembered God throughout the ages. Even if this remembering for others does not take place consciously, and people with dementia are not present in church services, the Church as Christ's body necessarily includes its weaker and absent members. As Paul says, they are 'indispensable' (1 Cor. 12:22). In the body of Christ,

> those members of the body that we think less honourable we clothe with greater honour, and our less respectable members are treated with greater respect. (1 Cor. 2:23)

Recounting our salvation in the liturgy always resonates with the hope we have of the completion of God's works in eternity.

---

[20] Ralph Kunz, 'Demenz als Metapher oder vom Glück und Elend des Vergessens', *Zeitschrift für Theologie und Kirche*, 111 (2014), 450.

[21] Kunz, 'Demenz als Metapher', 439.

In this way it is also a memory that is open to the future.[22] God's eternal time and our limited, earthly time cross in prayer and liturgy, and in a particular way in the Eucharist. For a moment, we are in the past, the present and the future at the same time. Our past redemption and our future completion have a bearing on our feeble hearts and souls of the present when we celebrate the liturgy and the Eucharist, together with and vicariously for people with dementia. This is a cognitive act and at the same time an act of love,[23] but it is also something that is only possible by God's grace. The Eucharist in particular reminds us that we are all fragile and in need of provisions for our journey through life. Celebrating it with people with dementia present, or in our thoughts and prayers, this experience is enhanced.[24]

Body Memory

People with dementia are not only included in the remembering of others, they have their own contribution to make. When we enter their world we realize that they *do* remember, sometimes in astonishing ways. Trying to cross the bridge as much as possible, we are able to make surprising discoveries.

We are all aware of the fact that our body remembers pain. This memory can be evoked when we enter a place in which we felt it before, e.g. a dentist's surgery. A place can link us to an experience unconsciously. Serious accidents, torture, or the threat of death may not be consciously remembered but are virulent in our memory and may be re-actualized in situations similar to that of the experienced trauma. But our body remembers much more than that: typing, reading, playing an

---

[22] Kunz, 'Demenz als Metapher', 439.

[23] Kunz, 'Demenz als Metapher', 452.

[24] See Regina Schlingheider, 'The Eucharist, Dementia and Time', *Journal of Religion, Spirituality & Aging*, 36:2 (2024), 181.

instrument or driving a car are examples of practiced habits we no longer think about. While we perform them we do not recall the details that we acquired in a long learning process. Yet all these skills are now available to us through a tacit memory of the body which unburdens us from an abundance of details.[25] Body memory is not a conscious retrieving of data and knowledge from the past but it *is* 'our lived past';[26] it is experience which has settled as a kind of sediment in our bodies, a manifestation of our life story. In the past, we also acquired certain gestures and expressions which we now employ without thinking, our *habitus*. The way we behave and interact with others is not performed consciously but acted out unconsciously with the help of a memory embedded and stored by our bodies, not unlike a sedimentation. 'Our entire personality is based on the memory of the body'.[27] So our body is not limbs and organs, movements and sensations only, but also a carrier of life history. This type of memory remains present when conscious memory goes and thus gives continuity to a life of a person with dementia. The presence of that latent experience can still be retrieved and will sometimes show itself unexpectedly.

A church member I visited in a care home did not recognize me, and conversation was not possible. But when I began to sing songs from the hymn book she sang with me, joining without apparent effort in many of the different verses. She had learned to sing these verses at some point in her life, and the capacity to sing them was still there. Thus she unconsciously integrated the past into the present situation, and some of her life history became

---

[25] Thomas Fuchs, 'The Phenomenology of Body Memory', in *Body Memory, Metaphor, and Movement*, ed. Sabine C. Koch, Thomas Fuchs, Michela Summa, and Cornelia Müller (John Benjamins, 2012), 13. https://tinyurl.com/7283-0193-1-1 (accessed 10 January 2025).

[26] Fuchs, 'Phenomenology', 11.

[27] Fuchs, 'Phenomenology', 15.

present. The body thus 'carries its own past into the surroundings as a procedural field of possibilities'.[28] Long after cognitive memory has gone, people with dementia have feelings, an ability to bond, and a sense of humour. They still have a personality. Nicci Gerrard writes about her father that when he had dementia, he was sometimes 'powerfully present ... He still had his sweetness; his past lived on in his smile, his frown, the way he raised his bushy silver eyebrows.'[29] Arno Geiger writes:

> In the poor man robbed of his senses, I often see my father as he once was. When he smiles at me, clear-eyed, which still happens a lot, thank goodness, I know that my visit was worthwhile for him, too. It's as if he doesn't know anything but understands everything.[30]

This underlines that there is a continuity in the personality of people with dementia and that they retain their body memory for a long time. They experience feelings such as shame, pride, and joy. They cause conflicts, which shows that they are still able to articulate their needs. They also retain a spiritual memory.[31]

Paul calls us to respect the weaker members of society more than those who are not weak. This may be because in doing so there is something that will benefit us, and we only discover this when we meet people with dementia on their own terms. While the forgetfulness of dementia may help us to form new relationships, it may also show us hitherto undiscovered qualities in that person. Like many families, ours at first did not realize that my mother had dementia. Looking back, I am not sure when it started, but I remember one day when we took a walk round my

---

[28] Fuchs, 'Phenomenology', 20.

[29] Nicci Gerrard, *What Dementia Teaches Us about Love* (Allen Lane, 2019), 3.

[30] Geiger, *The Old King in his Exile*, 180.

[31] This is examined below, 'Consider the lilies of the field', p. 21.

mother's garden. When we came to a gooseberry bush which was not quite straight my mother tried to alter its position, but said when she did not succeed: 'Well, let's leave it at that'. This was so untypical of my mother, who always needed to get things right, that this moment has remained in my memory very clearly. I think she was at the point of entering a world in which she would be more relaxed about things she could not influence any longer. This took away some of the fretfulness of life, not only for herself, but also for those around her.

In his book discussing the theological issues surrounding dementia, David Keck says that his mother, affected by Alzheimer's disease, 'can still teach us all about the love of God'.[32] Below I examine five aspects that show how people with dementia are sustained by God in this terrible illness and how they can live lives of faith which may help people without dementia.

'Fulfill the law of Christ.' (Gal 6:2):
   —Being a Burden

Progress in medicine means that many illnesses that used to be lethal can now be cured or treated in a way that makes them bearable. Some forms of cancer, for example, have lost their terror, and in many cases cancer is not equated with death as it was fifty years ago.[33] But the belief that every illness can be cured is an illusion. Dementia frees us from that illusion, as it is (presently) incurable.[34] It is not a new illness, but it is new on the huge scale

---

[32] David Keck, *Forgetting Whose We Are*, 5.

[33] In 1977, Susan Sontag wrote: '[T]oday, in the popular imagination, cancer equals death.' See Susan Sontag, *Illness as Metaphor and AIDS and Its Metaphors* (Picador, 1977), 7.

[34] There is medication to ease symptoms in certain types of dementia, especially in its early stages. See 'Medication for Dementia Symptoms', Alzheimer's Society, https://tinyurl.com/7283-0193-1-2 (accessed 10 January 2025). A fairly recent prescription approval is Leqembi, approved in the United States in 2023 and in the UK in 2024.

that we currently see it.[35] The burden on individual carers and on society is immense, and increases every year. Almost every family is affected by now and in some way burdened by it. As dementia cannot be cured, it forces us to care for those who are affected, often for a very long time. This aspect of the necessity of prolonged care is responsible for one of the greatest fears regarding becoming ill with dementia: the fear of being a burden to others. However, when we express the fear of being a burden we forget that being a burden is part of normal life. We are always dependent on others, 'to live is to be a burden'.[36] Self-sufficiency may be highly regarded, but it is not the norm. We are always bound to other humans in our needs, and we could not survive without them.[37] Moreover, no life can be led without suffering. This is true in a particular way for Christians. Throughout the ages the Church has been called to engage with suffering, and to practice solidarity with those who are on the margins. This is a natural part of being a Christian, if we believe Galatians 6:2: 'Bear one another's burdens, and in this way you will fulfil the law of Christ.' Following on from Galatians 5, this sentence is a call to love one's neighbours and to help them to carry their burdens. In a less obvious way, it is also about being one of those who are being carried—which may be the harder part, so being a burden to others may well be part of our Christian calling.

---

[35] Its first mention goes back to the thirteenth century. German psychiatrist Alois Alzheimer was the first who identified abnormal tangles and plaques in the brain of a woman suffering from memory loss in 1906. See 'Alois Alzheimer', Alzheimer's Disease International, https://tinyurl.com/7283-0193-1-3 (accessed 2 November 2024).

[36] Warren A. Kinghorn, '"I Am Still with You": Dementia and the Christian Wayfarer', *Journal of Religion, Spirituality & Aging*, 28/1–2 (2015).

[37] Living means 'being at each other's mercy.' See Gerrard, *What Dementia Teaches Us about Love*, 40.

Pope John Paul II, who suffered from Parkinson's disease, did not resign despite being seriously ill in his last years. He did not think he lost his dignity when he needed support to be able to appear in public. He believed that visible suffering was part of his ministry. He is reported to have said: 'Si crollo, crollo.'[38] At Easter 2005, shortly before his death, he was not able to speak due to a tracheotomy, but blessed the crowds from his apartment window.[39] For me, his courage to be a burden visibly to the public has a powerful message and points to the Christian ministry of suffering and of being someone who is cared for by others. It also highlights that people who are ill and disabled and deviate from what most perceive as the norm must be visible and part of public life. Not hiding those who suffer would benefit society as a whole and take away a lot of our fear about becoming disabled ourselves.

People with dementia must be visible because they remind us of our fragility and vulnerability. It is good to remember our limitations and our inadequacy before God. It is good to contemplate that ageing *does* mean disability, and that most of us will be old and variously disabled eventually.[40] As any ageing

---

[38] 'If I break down, I break down.'

[39] William B. Blakemore, 'St. John Paul II', *Britannica,* https://tinyurl.com /7283-0193-1-4 (accessed 25 May 2024).

[40] Jenni Dutton describes dementia as a 'difficult gift'. As cited in Gerrard, *What Dementia Teaches Us about Love,* 97. In a similar fashion, the Amish, a traditionalist protestant fellowship, believe that a disabled person is a special blessing from God. Visibility and integration are not discussed much, but traditionally practised. 'Because children and adults with congenital disorders and other disabilities live at home and find work within the community, they are an ever-present reminder to those with whom they live to slow down or modify routines and expectations, and to include those with different abilities in the tasks of everyday life.' See Erik Wesner, 'The Amish and Special Needs Children', https://tinyurl.com/7283-0193-1-5 (accessed 24 October 2024).

people, those with dementia hold us up and slow us down.[41] James Woodward reflects on an old man at a pedestrian crossing whose 'journey across the road seems to take forever'.

> As I drove off something very profound and disturbing struck me. He was me! … The old man had become a stark foreshadowing of what I would become. His vulnerability would become mine with all its dependence and imperfections … His ageing reflected my own.[42]

Frailty is not an exception but part of life, and awaiting most of us in our later lives. People with dementia remind us that we will be like them and that there is not so much difference between us even now. Nicci Gerrard writes that she and her husband 'often talk about what we would do if we got dementia':

> I'm struck that while both of us would want to accompany and care for the other — or we think that we would, which is something very different — we would not want to be looked after by the other, at the mercy of their kindness and the object of their pity and disgust.[43]

In Western societies there is great fear of being vulnerable and a great reluctance to ask for help. People with dementia can show us that being vulnerable is normal, that being helped by others is part of life, and that being a burden is a task awaiting most of us.

---

[41] Kate Swaffer, an Australian dementia activist, goes further by saying that '[p]utting people in homes is a form of segregation'. 'We don't have schizophrenia villages. We don't have cancer villages.' See Tory Shepherd, 'Why Kate Swaffer is Demanding Dementia Rights', *The Guardian*, 15 September 2024, https://tinyurl.com/7283-0193-1-6 (accessed November 11, 2024).

[42] James Woodward, 'Reimagining the Theology of Old Age', in *Spiritual Dimensions of Ageing*, ed. Malcolm Johnson and Joanna Walker (Cambridge University Press, 2016), 271.

[43] Nicci Gerrard, *What Dementia Teaches Us about Love*, 60–1.

'Someone else will fasten a belt around you' (John 21:18)
  —Handing Over

My sister-in-law, whose mother has dementia, shares looking after her with her sister. Her mother will stay with her for some weeks and then move to her other daughter's place for a while. This is difficult for her mother to grasp. Last time she left my sister-in-law's home she asked her: 'How much have you paid to get rid of me?'

As people with dementia increasingly fail to make sense of life around them and of what is happening to them, there is usually a great amount of suspicion. There are gaps of information that keep them from working out an unfamiliar situation, and these gaps may be filled with 'old or invented bits of information'.[44] This can be immensely stressful for the person with dementia and their carers. But there is often a later stage when people with dementia become able to trust those who look after them. Their worries cease, and they leave behind suspicions and barriers.

A friend's mother is known at her care home as someone you can have a good laugh with. The other day, one of the care workers told my friend that her mother had asked her for her age and she had suggested she gave a guess. 'Well, I think you must be getting on for ninety, now, like myself' the old woman said, and then both of them laughed merrily. This kind of behaviour is surprising in a woman who used to find life hard, nearly always worried and complained a lot. My friend tells me that her mother has stopped worrying now and feels content for most of the time. This has changed their relationship, too, which is much more relaxed than it was.

My friend says that her mother is in a good home where she is treated well. This contributes to her being able to relax and

---

[44] June Andrews, *Dementia: The One-Stop Guide* (Profile Books, 2015), 15.

crack jokes. People with dementia often have a good intuition about who can be trusted and who cannot.

Federica Caracciolo, who looked after her husband who had dementia, decided to take him home again after he had been in care for some time, and employed a carer to help her. Although life with her husband was hard and she did not get much sleep at night or rest during the day she says she never regretted her decision. With time, she noticed that her husband, who had been leading a rather independent life as a photographer for the United Nations, depended on her completely. Moreover, he trusted her. She writes:

> then I understood that I had become his only pillar of strength, his last rock, and that inspired in me a great desire to help him. He had given over his whole life to me and I felt joy and tenderness in offering him my support.[45]

Often, people with dementia know who they can trust, and they can show their trust in touching ways. The above example shows that this can make the hard task of caring for them easier. In John's Gospel, Jesus talks to his disciple Peter about his younger years when he 'used to fasten' his 'own belt' and chose his own ways. Then he looks into his future: 'when you grow old, you will stretch out your hands, and someone else will fasten a belt around you.' (John 21:18). The ability to let others do that and choose our ways for us is something we can learn from those people with dementia who do not mind others looking after them and who trust them completely. When they show us that they need us it touches something in us and helps us to discover ourselves in a new way. It shows that it can be worthwhile to risk this difficult relationship. We may grow with it and make new discoveries about ourselves and the things of which we are capable.

----

[45] Federica Caracciolo, *Alzheimer: A Journey Together* (Jessica Kingsley, 2006), 55.

'Consider the lilies of the field' (Matt. 6:28)
  — The Capacity to Enjoy Life

Christina Puchalski describes a moment when her mother who suffered from advanced dementia pointed out to her the beauty of the place where they were sitting: 'Look at the flowers and the ducks!' This reminded her daughter of the 'lilies of the field' (Matt. 6:28); she could feel God's presence, and sensed for a moment that 'the cares of us both had left'.[46]

For most of us, work is an important aspect of life. We enjoy getting things done, and the feeling of having achieved something makes us feel content and helps us see our lives as worth living. Being busy can make us happy and give us a sense of purpose, but it can also keep us from living life in its fullness. People with dementia show us aspects of life apart from busyness and help us consider whether we are putting too much emphasis on always having something to do.

When my mother had had dementia for some time but could still do a little gardening she used to say that while being out in the garden she felt somehow connected to the farmers working in the adjoining fields. She could hear their voices and the purring of their tractors. Her special delight were the children who were brought and who played in the corners of the fields there while their parents worked. As gardening used to be about getting things done, these are details she never noticed before. If she had, she would not have considered them worth mentioning. But when she had dementia, she often told me on the phone about this 'connecting' with life around her and whenever she did I could feel some of her joy at being alive and was able to share it. Apart from reassuring me that she was not unhappy it

---

[46] Christina Puchalski, 'Dementia: A Spiritual Journey for the Patient and the Caregivers', in *The Paradox of Disability*, ed. Hans S. Reinders (Eerdmans, 2010), 48.

reminded me that there were good things in store for me, even should life become less active and more restricted.

Moreover, the pressure to achieve and deliver is gone. When I was a child, my mother used to sing with us a lot, especially on walks through the countryside. She was particularly fond of rounds, and she would expect us to carry our tune and scold us if we didn't. I would not sing with my mother now if she did not have dementia, as I would still feel the pressure to achieve. But in the given circumstances it is something we can share and enjoy, with much laughing when one of us fails to carry her tune. It reconciles me a little to my childhood experience, and I enjoy discovering a much more relaxed mother from the one I knew before she had dementia.

Visiting his father in the care home, Arno Geiger talked him into arm-wrestling and let him win:

> He had fun, more on account of the 'nonsense' we were getting up to than because he won. He didn't comment on his wins, but said with a smirk, 'People doing what we're doing are hardly needed around here.'[47]

Geiger says that in the care home, his father 'felt good' among people like him. 'There are other good-for-nothing layabouts here. I've rounded up quite a crowd.'[48] His father, a hard-working man for all of his life, was aware of being 'useless' but was able to accept that fact with a sense of humour. People with dementia remind us of the biblical command to be useless from time to time.

> And why do you worry about clothing? Consider the lilies of the field, how they grow; they neither toil nor spin, yet I tell you, even Solomon in all his glory was not clothed like one of these. But if God so clothes the grass of the field, which is alive

---

[47] Geiger, *The Old King in his Exile*, 164.
[48] Geiger, *The Old King in his Exile*, 169.

today and tomorrow is thrown into the oven, will he not much more clothe you—you of little faith? Therefore do not worry, saying, "What will we eat?" or "What will we drink?" or "What will we wear?" (Matt. 6:28–31).[49]

There are times when God wants us not to be busy and worrying, but just to be. People with dementia can show us how to be royals who rest and feel connected with this world.[50] This helps us now, as people without dementia, to pause and take time out from our busy lives. It also helps us regarding our future. Maybe we do not have to fear dementia so much if we realize that there may be good things in store for us in our old age.

People with dementia are forced into a state of resting. Connecting with God and the world he has made may be made easier by not doing anything. It may also happen in a more direct way when thinking is of less importance. Wendy Mitchell relates how she was afraid of animals in childhood and how this changed when she had dementia. Her daughter's cat Billy now is her best friend.

> I've learned so much from animals. This change in my personality, this softening in one part of my brain, has meant that I've made time to sit and stop and watch, much like they do. Animals lead a simple life—they live in the moment, and that's what I've found I have in common with Billy, an appreciation of now.[51]

Other examples show that parts of our selves unexpectedly emerge when we have dementia. We may enjoy different things

---

[49] See also Eccl. 9:7: Go, eat your bread with enjoyment, and drink your wine with a merry heart; for God has long ago approved what you do.

[50] Arno Geiger concludes his book with the sentence: 'It's said that whoever waits long enough can become king.' *The Old King in his Exile*, 183.

[51] Wendy Mitchell, *Somebody I Used to Know* (Bloomsbury, 2018), 169.

compared to our lives before dementia. A friend of mine plays in a small chamber orchestra, and one day the room in which they usually rehearsed was not available. One of them who knew someone in a care home for senior residents, many of them ill with dementia, organized a room for them there. During the rehearsal more and more of the residents came in and listened to the music. Many stayed for a long time and would not leave even when they were called for dinner. As only a small percentage of our populace is interested in classical music, I assume only a few of them would have listened to it voluntarily before they had dementia. But they seemed to enjoy it now and did not appear to get bored with it. My friend felt that the music seemed to speak to something in them, and they must have thought it worthwhile to stay on and listen, even when they could have had dinner instead. Another aspect of their enjoyment may have been the fact that while listening they were not required to make conversation, which is often challenging to people with dementia. Yet there was communication, between the musicians and the listeners; there was a special form of connection with life, and possibly with eternity too. Singing may be the language of heaven, as Warren Kinghorn says: 'The end is music.'[52]

Being busy can be really good, but the Sermon on the Mount reminds us that there is more to life than that. We are asked to 'consider the lilies of the field' as they do not worry about tomorrow or strive for achievement. In times of rest, we may discover aspects of life hitherto unknown to us and connect with life in a new way. An appreciation of music may be such an example of the fullness of life which we may miss out on in lives where work never stops.

---

[52] Kinghorn, '"I Am Still With You"', 116.

'God chose what is foolish' (1 Cor. 1:27)
 —Relationships and Reconciliation

As people with dementia change, so relationships change with people around them. There is usually great sorrow about these changes, as the person we used to know seems to disappear more and more. We lose them, but as they are still alive, our loss is not clear. Pauline Boss has called it 'ambiguous loss'. We grieve for those we lose but it is a grief which remains unresolved and can be traumatic just because it is so uncanny and confusing.[53] Seeing someone you love changing into someone very different is one of the most difficult aspects of dementia. But relationships can alter in a positive way, too. Arno Geiger felt that being with his father was easier than it was before he became ill with dementia because former conflicts did not influence their relationship any longer. But he experienced more than that:

> There's something between the two of us that has led me to open myself more to the world. Which is, of course, the opposite of what people normally say that Alzheimer's does—that it cuts connections. Sometimes it creates them.[54]

Without having sorted out the things that had made it difficult, this relationship was now less complicated and more relaxed. And it gained a new importance as the son realized that his father was close to death and that each visit might be the last. 'It is a strange situation. Everything I give him, he can't hold onto. Everything he gives me, I hold onto with all my strength.'[55]

It was not only the closeness of death which made his father's comments so valuable to Geiger. He realized that there was wisdom in what his father said, and he wanted as much of

---

[53] See Pauline Boss, 'The Trauma and Complicated Grief of Ambiguous Loss', *Pastoral Psychology*, 59 (2010), 137.

[54] Geiger, *The Old King in his Exile*, 172.

[55] Geiger, *The Old King in his Exile*, 171.

it as he could get. It seems strange to expect wisdom from someone who has, in the eyes of many, become a fool, yet to Geiger
the words and actions of a father who could not think clearly
any longer developed an exceptional importance. 'It's as if he
doesn't know anything but understands everything.'[56]

People with dementia retain feelings and their ability to
bond long after cognitive memory goes. They do not remember
people they meet by name but rather by the way they feel about
them. They may forget faces, but a sense of who they feel com-
fortable with remains for a long time. Wendy Mitchell, a person
with dementia, is haunted by the idea that she may forget who
her daughters are one day. But she says: 'Even though you may
forget that your friends or family visited recently … what stays
with you are the feelings you had of love, happiness and comfort
when they were near.' She relates visiting a dementia support
group for the second time: 'There is no fear or hesitancy as I walk
in this morning, I might not remember the faces around the
table, but I remember that I felt very relaxed around them.'[57]

As thinking things through is no longer possible, emotions
may be of a much higher value in their lives. With other means
of assessing situations and people gone, intuition takes first
place. In certain circumstances, this can be seen not only as a loss
but also as a gain. French writer Jacques Lusseyran, who lost his
sight at the age of eight, insisted that he could still see, only in a
different way. He was grateful to his parents, 'for whom, above
all, it was not necessarily a curse to be different from other
people.' They were 'willing to admit that their way of looking
at things, the usual way, was perhaps not the only possible
one.'[58] In his family, his blindness was not seen as a loss, but as

---

[56] Geiger, *The Old King in his Exile*, 180.

[57] Mitchell, *Somebody I Used to Know*, 134.

[58] Jacques Lusseyran, *And There Was Light*, trans. Elizabeth R. Cameron
(Floris, 1985), 28.

a difference with possibilities. During World War II, Lusseyran formed a resistance group in Nazi-occupied France. When potential new group members were interviewed they would always have to go and 'see the blind man' as he would sense better than anyone else whether they were trustworthy or not.

For Lusseyran, light did not disappear but had a different quality. He relates how he found his way about 'by not thinking about it at all, or thinking as little as possible.'[59] It is worth trying to see dementia as a disability that enables people to see things differently and to point out things to us that as people without dementia we are not able to see.

It is astonishing how God sometimes speaks to us through the fine wisdom of people with dementia. My mother, who trained in Germany to be a typist during the war years, recently recounted how back then all the young apprentices would walk through the office during working hours singing Nazi songs. 'My boss couldn't do anything about it!' I was amazed that at this stage in her life, with an impaired memory, she reflected on the unfairness of what she did as a young girl. The necessity to defend those times against the accusations of her children was gone, and so was the harshness with which both parties argued when we were younger. Now, my mother seems to remember different aspects of her life with more compassion. This has changed my relationship with her and sometimes makes me reflect on my own harshness in judgment and lack of compassion in many things. I realize that, in a very different way from when were both younger, she has become my teacher.

Maybe it is what was described by Wendy Mitchell as a 'softening' of part of the brain which results in a different and more compassionate way of remembering.[60] It may lead to a kind of reconciliation with the past which a sound mind might

---

[59] Lusseyran, *And There Was Light*, 20.

[60] See above for the full quotation. Mitchell, *Somebody I Used to Know*, 169.

have prevented. People with dementia may say things a healthy person would not be able to figure out.[61] A less cognitive access to memory may result in more wisdom. This brings to mind 1 Cor 1:27: 'God chose what is foolish.' In certain situations God may choose people with dementia to reveal things to us which we could not have discovered without their wisdom.

'The kingdom of God is among you' (Luke 17:21) — Approaching Death

Dementia cannot be healed and will inevitably lead to death. The Bible calls us to contemplate death, as this will make us wise, but for us this is difficult advice.[62] We avoid death and do not want to think about life's transience. People with dementia may help us there as, for them, death often becomes part of life in a way that seems unreal to us at first. But if we are ready to pay attention to their experiences they may teach us something about dying and death.

As dementia progresses, there is an increasing loss of touch with the real world. Arno Geiger describes how he tries to keep his father connected with reality and how he learns with time to give up that battle. He understands at last that putting his father right when he talks about his long dead mother as if she were alive does not make things easier:

> Was she dead or alive? Who cares? It made no difference. Once I had accepted that my father was reviving the dead a little, and, in so doing, bringing himself a little closer to death, I managed to enter deeper into his suffering.[63]

For most people in old age, the dead seem to come closer in their thoughts. For people with dementia, who reflect on

---

[61] Kunz, 'Demenz als Metapher', 442.

[62] E.g. Ps. 90:12, Eccl. 3:1–2.

[63] Geiger, *The Old King in his Exile*, 58.

little, the dead are present in a real sense, and they tend to act accordingly. This behaviour seems odd to us, but being with the dead may be, for them, 'a home outside the tangible world.'[64] For us, their mixing up of the past and the present, of people who are dead with those who are alive, is just another sign of their decline. But for them it may well be a preparation for life after death.

When people with dementia revive the dead, it is not a stepping back into the past but rather a stepping aside into a kind of parallel world that is beyond time.[65] They become wanderers between reality and this other world, and from their point of view this is perfectly reasonable behaviour. Time stops being chronological, and different times fuse, as in the kingdom of God—which is something we move towards in the future, but which at the same time is present already: 'The kingdom of God is among you' (Luke 17:21).[66]

We have seen that in our lives of faith, the past, the present and the future can come together, especially during the Eucharist, as we re-enact the first Eucharist on the night before Jesus's death and anticipate the great banquet in heaven. When people with dementia meet those who have died, they take the past with them into the present, but they also anticipate seeing them again after they have died themselves. They do not reflect on this, and so the past and the future are present for them in a real sense. This can result in a mixing up of persons: on her deathbed, my aunt took me for my mother, her sister-in-law. Also, several people may merge into one single person. Matthias Lohenner describes his mother looking at him and saying: 'Dad

---

[64] Geiger, *The Old King in his Exile*, 15.

[65] Matthias Lohenner, *Wo kommst du denn her? Teilnehmende Beobachtung einer Demenz* (Wichern-Verlag, 2024), 99.

[66] This fusing of time in the Divine is discussed in Dumitru Stăniloae and Kallistos Ware, *Time*, Fairacres Publications 208 (SLG Press, 2023).

… Karl … children … you are all of them. And that is fine.'[67] The person she saw, her son, represented a whole range of persons, dead and alive, who merged 'into one single beloved and loving vis-à-vis'.[68]

Death can, for some people, become a person who visits us and walks with us during the last phase of life. In Eberhard Rathgeb's book *Das Paradiesghetto* an old woman not only meets her dead father in her thoughts but also death himself: 'Death looks rather friendly, when he sits next to me, and I think I can trust him. When he doesn't visit I start missing him.'[69] St Francis, in his 'Canticle of the Creatures' welcomes death as a sister. And I remember that in a talk at the Evangelische Akademie Baden in Bad Herrenalb, not long before she died, German theologian Dorothee Sölle said that death had become to her someone who lived close to her, in the next room.[70]

People with dementia spend much of their time in a world apart from our reality, they live in exile. This exile seems to be a place where meeting with the dead in an immediate way is possible. People with dementia do not travel into the past, the past is present for them now. The dead are alive. As strange as this may seem, it may have positive aspects, for us, too.

Exile is a hard place because it means you had to leave your home. But at the same time it can be a refuge when home has become a place where you do not find your way about any longer. The exile of people with dementia is a world in which certain things do not count, such as conflicts from the past: it is a world where there is some peace. Matthias

---

[67] Lohenner, *Wo kommst du denn her*, 107, my translation.

[68] Lohenner, *Wo kommst du denn her*, 107, my translation.

[69] Eberhard Rathgeb, *Das Paradiesghetto* (Carl Hanser Verlag, 2014), 187, my translation.

[70] I could not find records of this talk, but it must have taken place in 2002 or 2003.

Lohenner relates the story of a friend's father who had had difficulties in finding his place in his family after returning from World War II and had been troubled by his war experience all his life. When he had dementia his daughter felt that he was serene and peaceful as never before in his life. As he could not return to past phases in his life, the place where he experienced that peace must have been an altogether different place, a world in which barriers were removed and where relationships were as they should be.[71]

People with dementia may show us 'life proceeding between this world and the next'.[72] In their contact with a different world they may have experiences which make them more serene and content. And in that world, there may be different standards. Lohenner's friend's father had broken with his own father, a difficult person. When he had dementia he began to see his father in a different light. There was some kind of reconciliation now possible in this world parallel to reality.[73]

The world we live in is troubled by its difficulties with relationships, our world is torn by conflict and war. In his poem 'Utopia' German poet Hanns Dieter Hüsch makes reference to a different world which may be the world anticipated to some extent by those with dementia:

> It is a time that I won't live to see,
> It is a world that's not of our world.
> It is a finely woven fabric,
> And friends, believe and see: it holds.[74]

---

[71] Lohenner, *Wo kommst du denn her*, 106.

[72] Angelika U. Reutter, as cited in Lohenner, *Wo kommst du denn her*, 108, my translation.

[73] Lohenner, *Wo kommst du denn her*, 109.

[74] My translation. See Hanns Dieter Hüsch, 'Utopie', hüsch.org, https://tinyurl.com/7283-0193-1-7 (accessed 6 February 2025).

It is encouraging to imagine a place and time where relationships are as they were meant by God to be. Perhaps the exile of people with dementia can at times be such a place, and a foreshadowing of eternity when we will all be reconciled and sit next to each other at the great banquet table.

Living and Praying with Trust

I remember being impressed, as a young student, by Socrates's alleged saying: 'The unexamined life is not worth living'.[75] It seemed to ring true then, but I am not so sure now whether a full life may not be possible without cognitive reflection. Perhaps people with dementia *do* examine life, albeit in a different manner. They seem to contemplate life intuitively, with astonishing results. There is humour, there is compassion, there is trust, and there is understanding.[76] People with dementia seem to know things, even if they can barely express this in words.

Knowing is not a cognitive process only, knowledge is not always expressed in words. Indeed words can 'get in the way of knowing'.[77] If we believe that 'the Word became flesh' (John 1:14), as the Bible tells us, reflection and cognition could be less important to our Christian faith than we presume. It is a faith in someone who 'lived among us' (John 1:14), and we are called to acknowledge that the person Jesus is the manifestation of God's Word. This means that not only Scripture, but that his life in human flesh, too, forms a basis for our faith. This is irrational, and our intellect is challenged by having to believe in someone who lived among us as God. There is something crazy

---

[75] Plato, *Apology*, section 38a, Perseus Digital Library, https://tinyurl.com/7283-0193-1-8 (accessed 12 January 2025).

[76] See Geiger, *The Old King in his Exile*, 180.

[77] Malcolm Goldsmith, 'When Words Are No Longer Necessary: The Gift of Ritual', *Journal of Religious Gerontology*, 12 (2002), 142.

about our faith.[78] Moreover, Jesus's ministry was not about words only: he visited people and shared time with them. He used non-verbal communication, especially when healing someone.[79] He did not only minister by words and deeds but also by simply being there.[80]

If we believe in a 'Word' that 'became flesh', faith is much more than thinking things through and getting our theology right. As Christians, we are called to meet God apart from words and theological concepts. Those who have impaired cognitive abilities and are considered fools by the world can help us with this, they can be our teachers.

Living with Trust

Far from denying the 'stress that sometimes became unbearable' Federica Caracciolo was able to see caring for her husband as a blessing 'Seldom in the past had I known such fullness of life, with no doubts as to the reason for my actions.'[81] This was possible because her husband trusted her completely. Caracciolo talks about a 're-invented' life for him, which he, with time, accepted without question, which made caring for him easier.[82] He lived a life of trust, totally different from the very independent life he had before dementia. Valuing independence more than

---

[78] Paul is well aware of this, e.g. in Rom. 1:16 when acknowledging that there may be shame about the Gospel or in 1 Cor. 1:18–25 when talking about a wisdom different from the wisdom of the world.

[79] See e.g. Mark 7:31–7 or Mark 8:22–6, where Jesus uses his saliva and the touch of his hands to heal a deaf and a blind man respectively.

[80] After stilling a storm, Jesus says to his disciples 'Why are you afraid? Have you still no faith?' meaning they could have taken courage before he stilled the storm simply because he was with them. See Mark 4:35–40.

[81] Caracciolo, *Alzheimer: A Journey Together*, 100.

[82] Caracciolo, *Alzheimer: A Journey Together*, 47.

most other things, it is our great fear that we might become a burden for others, or that others might become a burden for us which we cannot cope with. Caracciolo's example shows that either can be part of our calling and may lead us into a life with a purpose that we did not expect.

People with dementia show us that it is possible to live with trust, they can also help us to trust more when we pray. They may not be able to talk with God as they used to; they may not be able to express themselves in prayer in so many words; but I believe that they can teach people without dementia important things about prayer.

Holy Moments

There are moments in life when we cannot pray. During the first weeks after my husband's death I was unable to sit down to pray for any length of time and could not say more than short sentences, such as 'Help me' or 'Hold me'. As time went on, I discovered formal prayer as a railing I could cling to, and I was greatly helped by the liturgy of the hours, especially a shortened version of Compline. It seemed to contain everything that was needed when I felt too vulnerable and too stressed to think about things I wanted to say to God. I could not think myself then, but others had thought up words for me which I could make use of. Moreover, I did not have to reflect on every word I said or sang during Compline. Nevertheless, it was prayer. And in this prayer I felt connected to those who prayed it in so many places all over the world at the same time as I did and to those who had prayed it throughout all the centuries of its existence.

I was held in that fabric of prayer across time and space. In a similar way, if we pray with people with dementia, they are held and supported in that fabric. They are not able to think as they used to, but that does not mean they cannot pray. Praying formal prayers with them may connect them with moments they had with God in the past, even if they do not remember them consciously or express them verbally. The first words of a well-known prayer or part of a liturgy can trigger body memory and lead them into joining with others in saying the familiar words. Elizabeth MacKinlay writes about a woman with rapidly advancing dementia to whom church had always been important. With the support of the other members, she still sang in the church choir and was brought by her husband to church services.

> One day, as the priest began the Great Thanksgiving Prayer, this woman spoke it with him, word for word. There was a sense of awe as we listened. She might not have been able to remember many things of her daily life, but with the thanksgiving prayer she spoke she seemed to enter into the experience of that sacred moment.[83]

'There was a sense of awe as we listened.' People with dementia can help us experience holy moments in prayer. There is spiritual memory in their world, not everything is loss and decline. And by the way they remember spiritually they remind us of God's grace and kindle the hope in us that even if we forget many things, God will not forget us.

Moments of Rest

When I visited my mother after an operation, she was restless and disorientated, but became calmer when we sang songs from the hymn book together. Before I left, I suggested we pray the Our Father. With me, she said the familiar words, and when we had finished, I felt that something had changed. My mother was completely calm, and we just held each other by

---

[83] Elizabeth MacKinlay, 'Journeys with People who Have Dementia: Connecting and Finding Meaning in the Journey', *Journal of Religion, Spirituality & Aging*, 28 (2016), 34.

the hands, looking into each other's eyes for quite some time.
It was a precious moment in which I felt we were connected,
with heaven and with each other. Reflecting on this on my
journey home I was amazed that we could pray together at all.
This would have been quite impossible before she had dementia—it would have been too embarrassing for both of us. As
my mother used to be a very active person before she had dementia, it was equally astonishing that we could just sit,
holding each other by the hand without doing anything else. I
realized that this moment could not have happened if she had
not had dementia.

Simple Asking

In my work, I try to prepare my sermons well and to avoid su-
perficiality in prayer. But I have noticed that these concerns lose
their importance when I am with a person with dementia. As in
other aspects of life, the pressure to achieve is gone and there is
no need to impress them. Likewise, when I am with them I feel
no need to impress God. They teach me that it is possible to talk
to God simply, and that being able to think clearly is not a pre-
requisite for prayer. In a study by Karen MacKinlay a man with
dementia was asked how he prayed, and he answered: 'I just say
well … I've got a problem and I'd appreciate your help if you
can.'[84] A woman with dementia said: 'I talk to God and tell him
to get organised, or is that me get organised.'[85] People with dementia have no concern for conventions; they talk to God as one
talks to a friend and name their immediate needs.[86] They may
do this in ways and words so unexpected that we may fear for

---

[84] Karen MacKinlay, 'Listening to People with Dementia: A Pastoral
   Care Perspective', *Journal of Religious Gerontology*, 13:3–4 (2003), 98.
[85] MacKinlay, 'Listening', 93.
[86] See Ex. 33:11, where God talks to Moses 'as a man speaks to his friend'.

God and the reverence due to him.[87] But perhaps people with dementia can teach us to see more clearly that God *is* our friend and that he *will* listen to our immediate needs. Jesuit priest and spiritual director Anthony de Mello reminds us that the key to prayer is simple asking. He recalls being told during a retreat:

> The key to the art of prayer is the prayer of petition ... The hand outstretched to beg obtains what the hand pressed against one's head to think does not.[88]

People with dementia remind me of this key to prayer. When I am with them, I do not have to think up clever phrases, I do not need to leave an impression. I can just be, and sense something of the rest that Jesus promised us.

> Come to me, all you that are weary and are carrying heavy burdens, and I will give you rest. (Matt. 11:28)

Getting Home

In group work with people with dementia, group members were asked what they thought God was like. One man answered: 'The Bible will take me home.'[89] This is an unusual answer to the question and it seems to lack logic. And yet I love that sentence because it is full of trust. It trusts that God gave us the Bible, his word, as something to hold on to on our way through this life. It trusts that he has prepared a home for us in eternity and that he will provide means to make sure we get there when our time comes. There is trust in this man's description of God, and it helps me to believe in Jesus' words:

---

[87] Malcolm Goldsmith, 'Through a Glass Darkly: A Dialogue between Dementia and Faith', *Journal of Religious Gerontology*, 12 (2002), 126.

[88] Anthony de Mello, *Contact with God* (Loyola University Press, 1991), 47.

[89] MacKinlay, 'Listening', 34.

In my Father's house there are many dwelling places. If it
were not so, would I have told you that I go to prepare a place
for you?   (John 14:2)

Even if I cannot read the Bible any longer, it is still there as
a token of God's love for me and it will 'take me home'. Maybe
when I have dementia and cannot rely on myself any longer my
reliance on God will increase and I can leave more and more of
my life to him.

WHAT PEOPLE WITH DEMENTIA TEACH US

By their vulnerability people with dementia teach us the basic Christian truth that we can only survive in community. They also remind us of important aspects of life that we may ignore because we are too clever or too busy. They teach us to slow down and take notice of the moment we are in. Moreover, they show us a different way of being together. Due to a 'softening' of their minds, our relationships with them become simpler and less demanding than they used to be. There is more humour when we are with them, we become more relaxed. We experience small moments of grace, and there is unanticipated reconciliation, as our conflicts are not remembered by them and thus have no bearing on the present. With them, we can take time out from the demands of life and enjoy the 'uncomplicated warmth' of someone who may not have been so easy to be with before.[90] As connectors of two worlds, reality and exile, people with dementia teach us about death. It is natural to them to re-vive the dead they meet in exile, in this parallel world that is real for them. This can help people without dementia to learn something about death and be less afraid of it.

When we pray with them, we notice how helpful formal prayer can be in times of need. With them, we say prayers we have known from childhood and are taken into a fabric of prayer across time and space. Together with them, we can experience rest in the presence of God which is often impossible in our busy lives without dementia. With them, we learn afresh that prayer

---

[90] Geiger, *The Old King in his Exile*, 72.

is about asking and that there is no need to impress God. With them, we learn to trust that God will find means to bring us home when our time comes.

Estonian composer Arvo Pärt once said that moments of perplexity are good moments and that 'you have to make peace with your helplessness. Then you will be given something that is like a gift.'[91] This is the dimension of trust we are called to as believers. People with dementia practice this in faith and prayer and we need them to be our teachers.

---

[91] My translation. Arvo Pärt, *Auf den Spuren eines estnischen Komponisten* tinyurl.com/7283-0193-1-9 (accessed 12 December 2025).

Bibliography

Alzheimer's Disease International. 'Alois Alzheimer' (17 August 2020).
https://www.alzint.org/about/dementia-facts-figures/types-of-dementia/alzheimers-disease/alois-alzheimer

Alzheimer's Society. 'Medication for Dementia Symptoms.' (17 January 2023).
https://www.alzheimers.org.uk/about-dementia/treatments/dementia-medication/medication-dementia-symptoms

Andrews, June, *Dementia: The One-Stop Guide* (Profile Books, 2015).

Blakemore, William B., 'St. John Paul II', *Britannica* (24 November 2025).
https://www.britannica.com/biography/Saint-John-Paul-II

Bonhoeffer, Dietrich, *Letters and Papers from Prison*, Dietrich Bonhoeffer Works in English vol. 8, ed. John W. de Gruchy, trans. Isabel Best, Lisa E. Dahill, Reinhard Krauss and Nancy Lukens (Fortress Press, 2010).

Boss, Pauline, 'The Trauma and Complicated Grief of Ambiguous Loss', *Pastoral Psychology*, 59 (2010), 137–145.
DOI: 10.1007/s11089-009-0264-0

Caracciolo, Federica, *Alzheimer: A Journey Together* (Jessica Kingsley, 2006).

De Mello, Anthony, *Contact with God* (Loyola University Press, 1991).

Fuchs, Thomas, 'The Phenomenology of Body Memory', in *Body Memory, Metaphor, and Movement*, ed. Sabine C. Koch, Thomas Fuchs, Michela Summa, and Cornelia Müller (John Benjamins, 2012).
https://www.klinikum.uni-heidelberg.de/fileadmin/zpm/psychatrie/fuchs/Literatur/The_phenomenology_of_body_memory.pdf

Geiger, Arno, *Der alte König in seinem Exil* (Carl Hanser Verlag, 2011.
——, *The Old King in his Exile*, trans. Stefan Tobler, (Carl Hanser Verlag, 2013).

Gerrard, Nicci, *What Dementia Teaches Us about Love* (Allen Lane, 2019).

Goldsmith, Malcolm, 'Through a Glass Darkly: A Dialogue between Dementia and Faith', *Journal of Religious Gerontology*, 12 (2002), 123–38.

    ☑ DOI: https://doi.org/10.1300/J078v12n03_10

——, 'When Words Are No Longer Necessary: The Gift of Ritual', *Journal of Religious Gerontology*, 12 (2002), 139–50.

    ☑ DOI: https://doi.org/10.1300/J078v12n03_11

——, *In a Strange Land: People with Dementia and the Local Church* (4M Publications, 2004).

Healey, Emma, *Elizabeth is Missing* (Penguin, 2015).

Hüsch, Hanns Dieter, 'Utopie', Hanns Dieter Hüsch im Internet (undated).

    ☑ http://www.hüsch.org/html/utopie.html

Keck, David, *Forgetting Whose We Are: Alzheimer's Disease and the Love of God* (Abingdon Press, 1996).

Kinghorn, Warren A., '"I Am Still with You": Dementia and the Christian Wayfarer', in *Journal of Religion, Spirituality & Aging*, 28/1–2 (2015), 98–117.

    ☑ DOI: 10.1080/15528030.2015.1046633

Kunz, Ralph, 'Demenz als Metapher oder vom Glück und Elend des Vergessens', *Zeitschrift für Theologie und Kirche*, 111 (2014), 437–53.

    ☑ DOI: 10.1628/004435414X14135326006031

——, 'Das Schicksal Demenz und Hiobs Botschaft', in *Kulturen der Sorge: Wie eine Gesellschaft ein Leben mit Demenz ermöglichen kann*, ed. Harm-Peer Zimmermann (Campus Verlag, 2018), 153–62.

Lohenner, Matthias, *Wo kommst du denn her? Teilnehmende Beobachtung einer Demenz* (Wichern-Verlag, 2024).

Lusseyran, Jacques, *And There Was Light*, trans. Elizabeth R. Cameron (Floris, 1985).

MacKinlay, Elizabeth, 'Journeys with People who Have Dementia: Connecting and Finding Meaning in the Journey', *Journal of Religion, Spirituality & Aging*, 28 (2016), 24–36.

MacKinlay, Karen, 'Listening to People with Dementia: A Pastoral Care Perspective', *Journal of Religious Gerontology*, 13:3–4 (2003), 91–106.
  DOI: 10.1300/J078v13n03_07

Mitchell, Wendy, *Somebody I Used to Know* (Bloomsbury, 2018).

Plato, *Apology*, Perseus Digital Library (undated).
  https://www.perseus.tufts.edu/hopper/text?doc=plat.+apol.+38a

Pärt, Arvo, 'Auf den Spuren eines estnischen Komponisten', *Taizé Archives*, Tallinn 2024 (1 October 2024).
  https://archives.taize.fr/de_article39360.html

Puchalski, Christina, 'Dementia: A Spiritual Journey for the Patient and the Caregivers', in *The Paradox of Disability*, ed. Hans S. Reinders (Eerdmans, 2010).

Rathgeb, Eberhard, *Das Paradiesghetto* (Carl Hanser Verlag, 2014).

Rohr, Richard, *Falling Upward: A Spirituality for the Two Halves of Life* (Jossey-Bass, 2011).

Schlingheider, Regina, 'The Eucharist, Dementia and Time', *Journal of Religion, Spirituality & Aging*, 36:2 (2024), 173–87.
  DOI: 10.1080/15528030.2023.2183304

Shepherd, Tory, 'Why Kate Swaffer is Demanding Dementia Rights', *The Guardian*, 15 September 2024.
  https://www.theguardian.com/australia-news/2024/sep/15/australia-dementia-awareness-kate-swaffer

Sontag, Susan, *Illness as Metaphor and AIDS and its Metaphors* (Picador, 1977).

Stăniloae, Dumitru and Kallistos Ware, *Time*, Fairacres Publications 208 (SLG Press, 2023).

Wesner, Erik, 'The Amish and Special Needs Children', *Amish America* (9 April 2013).
  https://amishamerica.com/amish-special-needs-children

Whitman, Lucy, ed., *People with Dementia Speak Out* (Jessica Kingsley Publishers, 2016).

Woodward, James, 'Reimagining the Theology of Old Age', in *Spiritual Dimensions of Ageing*, ed. Malcolm Johnson and Joanna Walker (Cambridge University Press, 2016), 271–81.

    DOI: https://doi-1org-1000034wmo6ob.erf.sbb.spk-berlin.de/10.1017/9781316136157

Films

Zeller, Florian, director, *The Father* (Les Films du Cru et al., 2020), 1'38".

Glatzer, Richard and Wash Westmoreland, directors, *Still Alice* (Killer Films and others, 2014), 1'39".

SLG PRESS PUBLICATIONS

FP1   *Prayer and the Life of Reconciliation*   Gilbert Shaw (1969)

FP2   *Aloneness not Loneliness*   Mother Mary Clare SLG (1969)

FP4   *Intercession*   Mother Mary Clare SLG (1969)

FP8   *Prayer: Extracts from the Teaching of Father Gilbert Shaw*   Gilbert Shaw (1973)

FP12   *Learning to Pray*   Mother Mary Clare SLG (1970, rev. 3/2025)

FP15   *Death, the Gateway to Life*   Gilbert Shaw (1971, 3/2024)

FP16   *The Victory of the Cross*   Dumitru Stăniloae (1970, 3/2023)

FP26   *The Message of Saint Seraphim*   Irina Gorainov (1974)

FP28   *Julian of Norwich: Four Studies to Commemorate the Sixth Centenary of the Revelations of Divine Love*   Sister Benedicta Ward SLG, Sister Eileen Mary SLG, Sister Mary Paul SLG, A. M. Allchin (1973, 3/2022)

FP43   *The Power of the Name: The Jesus Prayer in Orthodox Spirituality*   Kallistos Ware (1974)

FP46   *Prayer and Contemplation* and *Distractions are for Healing*   Robert Llewelyn (1975, rev. 4/2025)

FP48   *The Wisdom of the Desert Fathers*   trans. Sister Benedicta Ward SLG (1975)

FP50   *Letters of Saint Antony the Great*   trans. Derwas Chitty (1975, 2/2021)

FP54   *From Loneliness to Solitude*   Roland Walls (1976)

FP55   *Theology and Spirituality*   Andrew Louth (1976, rev. 1978, 3/2024)

FP61   *Kabir: The Way of Love and Paradox*   Sister Rosemary SLG (1977)

FP62   *Anselm of Canterbury: A Monastic Scholar*   Sister Benedicta Ward SLG (1973, 2/2024)

FP67   *Mary and the Mystery of the Incarnation: An Essay on the Mother of God in the Theology of Karl Barth*   Andrew Louth (1977, 2/2024)

FP68   *Trinity and Incarnation in Anglican Tradition*   A. M. Allchin (1977, rev. 2/2025)

FP70   *Facing Depression*   Gonville ffrench-Beytagh (1978, 2/2020)

FP71   *The Single Person*   Philip Welsh (1979)

FP72   *The Letters of Ammonas, Successor of St Antony*   trans. Derwas Chitty, introd. Sebastian Brock (1979, 2/2023)

FP74   *George Herbert, Priest and Poet*   Kenneth Mason (1980)

FP75   *A Study of Wisdom: Three Tracts by the Author of The Cloud of Unknowing*   trans. Clifton Wolters (1980)

FP81   *The Psalms: Prayer Book of the Bible*   Dietrich Bonhoeffer, trans. Sister Isabel SLG (1982, rev. 3/2025)

FP82   *Prayer & Holiness: The Icon of Man Renewed in God*   Dumitru Stăniloae (1982, rev. 2/2023)

FP85   *Walter Hilton: Eight Chapters on Perfection & Angels' Song*   trans. Rosemary Dorward (1983, rev. 3/2024)

FP88   *Creative Suffering*   Iulia de Beausobre (1989)

FP90   *Bringing Forth Christ: Five Feasts of the Child Jesus by St Bonaventure*   trans. Eric Doyle OFM (1984, 3/2024)

FP92   *Gentleness in John of the Cross*   Thomas Kane (1985, rev. 2/2025)

FP94   *Saint Gregory Nazianzen: Selected Poems*   trans. John McGuckin (1986, 2/2024)

FP95   *The World of the Desert Fathers: Stories and Sayings from the Anonymous Series of the Apophthegmata Patrum*   trans. Columba Stewart OSB (1986, 2/2020)

FP104   *Growing Old with God*   Timothy N. Rudd (1988, 2/2020)

FP106   *Julian Reconsidered*   Kenneth Leech, Sister Benedicta Ward SLG (1988, rev. 2/2024)

FP108   *The Unicorn: Meditations on the Love of God*   Harry Galbraith Miller (1989)

www.slgpress.co.uk